Motivation

To make it

Through

LISA SOLOMON

DEDICATION

This book is dedicated to the memory of my beloved mother, Carolyn Goosby Coleman, who died when I was 10 years old. I let nothing stop me mom and this one is for you.

I pray an abundance of blessings repose upon your life!

Love,
Lisa

ACKNOWLEDGEMENTS

First and foremost, I want to thank God for giving me the wisdom and understanding to give words of life, encouragement, and motivation. Without God in my life, I'm nothing! He is the TRUE author and finisher of my Faith!

Thank you to my beautiful daughters, Daphene and DeLisha. When my days were dark you both gave me a reason to get back up again! It warms my heart to know that I raised such smart, intelligent and awesome young ladies! I gave birth to you, but you both gave life to me!

My husband, My King, A True Man of God, John Lewis Solomon Jr., I love you! Thank you for standing beside me throughout the writing of this book. You've been my inspiration and motivation for continuing to improve my knowledge and move forward in my calling! Thanks for sharing in my happiness when starting this project and following with encouragement when it seemed too difficult to complete. Thanks for not only believing, but knowing that I could do this! I Love You Always & Forever!

To my "Kool" stepson, Linwood Gannt, I love you! You compliment me even on the days when I'm not looking my best, lol! Thank you for being the "light" to my day! Continue to be the bright and strong young man, I know you to be!

My Awesome author friends, Shana Johnson Burton and Allison Randall Berewa. I've learned so much from you two! Shana, if it wasn't for you critiquing one of my books, I wouldn't have known how to start a good book. Thank you, chick, for being a friend when I needed one. Allison, my child-hood friend! What can I say? You've been such an encourager to me! You helped me when no one else was there, and I'll forever be grateful! I pray blessings and much love to you both!

Mia Corey, Linda Crowell, Sharlene Exum, and Tangie Franks...Oh, how I love you all! Mia, you were the shoulder I leaned on and you were always a friend indeed. Thank you! You had to hear my cries over the years and you never judged me! Linda, you always kept it real with me....no sugar-coating! I listened! I will finish the book we started and you will get the first copy, lol! Tangie, your sweet spirit always lifted me up. Your smile, always let me know that everything would be alright! Sharlene, over 25-years we've been friends! You've always been there and we've been through a lot! Whew! Praise God we made it!

Tonja Harden, Mary Johnson, Cristy Henderson Reid, and Travon Sears......thank you for saving my life! Without each of you, I would NOT be here today! You will forever be my "Four Angels!" May God, bless you and your families continuously! I love you!

To my friend Kesha Garvin, thank you for all your love and support. You are a true friend who brings nothing but the Truth and always keeping it Real! That means so much to me! I pray God bless you and your family ABUNDANTLY!!

To each of my Facebook friends, thank you for your encouragement and blessings since 2009! I have a terrific group of friends and I ask God to bless each of you abundantly!

To my family and friends, thanks for believing in me and loving me! The prayers and kindness you have shown me over the years are appreciated!

Forever Grateful, *Lisa Denise Solomon*

FOREWORD

I have come to admire this woman, who is my wife, and she continues to impress me by her heartfelt words and acts of kindness towards others, that moved me initially. I have also found that the very words and spirit she employs to motivate others, she also embraces to strengthen and improve her own life. Despite fighting a daily battle against Lupus, she continues to push herself to press forward and be the best that she can be.

In this her book ***Motivation To Make It Through***, she gives some of her most powerful

inspiring rhetoric that moves you to tears, lifts your heart and causes your soul to soar to higher heights, infused with a won't quit, won't stop, you can do it attitude.

Her prayers in this book are amazingly personal and offer a heart to heart monologue with a loving Father God in the similitude of King David in the Psalms. And you will discover, as I did, that the "maximized moments" are right now epochs that should be approached in the spirit of "carpe per diem!" As an author of several books and an apostle, I implore you to take her quotes and motivation literally because she is not speaking from things she overheard, but rather she is speaking from a place of divine breathed inspiration, from personal pain, from perseverance, from purpose, and from power. May this book leave you **Motivated To Make It Through**!

Apostle John L. Solomon

Preface

1st Step-As I stand at the bottom of the steps, suicidal thoughts consume my mind. They are deeper than my mind can hold. I look up and I see the "Stage." What is the Stage? On the stage, I see my blessings...victory, deliverance, healing, peace of mind, joy... And LIFE. My inner-being reached out to climb the steps to get to the "Stage," but my "deeper thoughts" said, "NO, kill yourself take your life!" God speaks to me and says, "But they that wait upon the LORD shall renew their strength; they shall mount up with wings as eagles; they shall run, and not be weary, and they shall walk, and not faint." I climb slowly up three more steps.

4th Step-As I stand on the 4th step, I look back at depression, worry, stress, heartache and low self-esteem. It seemed easier to just go back and give up as doubt tells me to, but God says to me; "And let us not be weary in well doing: for in due season we shall reap, if we faint not." I CAN DO THIS! With that, I climbed four more steps.

8th Step-As I stand on the 8th step, I'm feeling my strength coming back. God has brought me out of tribulation before; I need to believe that He can do it again! I heard a voice speak to me and say, "The things which are impossible with men are possible with God." I CAN NOW CLIMB THE REST OF THE STEPS TO MY VICTORY, DELIVERANCE, HEALING, PEACE OF MIND, JOY, and MY LIFE!

THE STAGE-As I stand on this stage, I cry tears of joy because I know God has a great work for me to do!

My message to you: When you feel that you want to quit and give up, don't, keep your FAITH in GOD! Go on and tell that devil to go sit down somewhere because of the Blood of Jesus covering you. God can turn your WORST experience into your GREATEST testimony!! I pray my testimony helps and blesses someone! My words are to motivate, encourage and help you to find strength in the time of need. Putting God first and foremost in your life refreshes your spirit, rejuvenates your mind, and provides healing for your body.

TABLE OF CONTENT

MY PERSONAL MOTIVATION

"*Did you know they are about to get their house taken away? They had no business buying that expensive house!*"

"*Girl, All four of her children got different baby daddies! She is a *#$!?@ !!*".

"*That guy did crack cocaine at one time! He got the nerve to call himself a preacher.*"

"*Wow, their lights got turned off today, they're so broke!*"

Sounds like GOSSIP! Why would you slander someone's name? Who are we to judge anyone? Why do you continue to be the person on the job, at church, and on the streets who tell EVERYBODY'S business? Pray for people don't tear them down! You have no idea what they have been through, or what they presently may be going through! Don't be a part of the teardown "street committee!" Why do you want accolades for being the first one to tell someone else's business? Be a blessing to others and not a hindrance!

Much Love!

I PRAISE and THANK GOD that the worse which could've happened didn't happen! I'm so glad God blocked it! He didn't allow the worse to happen through all you've gone through! YOU KNOW WHY? BECAUSE NO WEAPON FORMED AGAINST ME OR YOU SHALL PROSPER and all things will work out for our good when we love God and are called to HIS purpose!!

"Well, I'll exercise one day, I just don't feel like it right now.

"Come to church with you, Oh, I'll be there next month."

"I know my son wants me to spend some time with him...but he'll be alright, we'll do something together in about two weeks."

"Yes I know the test is in the morning, but I'll study when I get to class."
"No, I'll call my mother another day...what? I didn't know she was sick!"

Sounds like PROCRASTINATION: "the act of willfully delaying the doing of something important that should and needs to be done." Most of us procrastinate from time-to-time, but it can become a self-sabotaging bad habit. Why put off for tomorrow for what you can do today? Ecclesiastes 9:10 says, "Whatsoever thy hand finds to do, do it with thy might; for there is no work, nor device, nor knowledge, nor wisdom, in the grave, where you one day will go." Tomorrow is not promised. Whatever you are called to do, need to do and want to do, do it NOW! If God has put something in your hands and heart to do, there should not be a delay in getting it done. I pray God give you the motivation to do today, what needs to be done today! Be a blessing to someone!

"Weeping may endure for a night, but joy comes in the morning!" Psalm 30:5. I remember going through different situations, being depressed, ready to quit, contemplating how to end it all, crying all night long... but it was just something about when the morning came.......GLORY.......I had so much PEACE!! Jesus said His yoke is easy and his burden is light! Confess how you feel your, fears, doubts, and anxieties. Tell Him, He already knows, he is waiting for you to confess it! THEN SURRENDER! LET IT GO! LEAVE IT WITH HIM! LET HIM TAKE IT! THEN WALK AWAY FROM IT! Don't give God the problem and then take it back! BE PATIENT! I always say, "God Got This!" JUST HOLD ON! YOU HAVE THAT ROPE, AND YOU THINK YOU'RE SLIPPING......YOU BETTER GRAB IT A LITTLE BIT TIGHTER HONEY, BECAUSE GOD AIN'T (Yes, in my country voice), "GOD AIN'T ", THROUGH WITH YOU YET!!!! YOU BETTER PRAISE HIM!

I DON'T LOOK LIKE, WHAT I'VE BEEN THROUGH!! You never know what people have been through... be hesitant to judge and show them some love! Thank God that He continues to cover us in HIS GLORY so that we don't look like what we could've looked like! Singing, "AFTER ALL THE THINGS I'VE BEEN THROUGH, I STILL HAVE JOY!!" I don't know about you but I got a reason to PRAISE HIM! There is a TRUE story behind MY PRAISE! My story may not be your story and your story may not be mine......but WE have a reason behind OUR PRAISE! You made it through the last "thing" and you WILL make it through this too!! I pray blessings upon you!

What use to be my struggle, has now become my Stepping Stone and my Strength! If we stop because of a hurdle or become afraid of the stumbling block, the destination will be blocked!!! Start thanking God for the struggles.... they will be your Stepping Stones to take you where God has destined you to go! All things will work together for your good! What was sent to take you under, God is using to take you OVER!!! Believe Blessings are coming to you!

I think often about how good God has already been to me. He made a way when there was no way, He healed me when I was sick, when the doctor said I was dying, He raised me up, He protected me without a mom/dad, opened doors when it seemed like all doors were close, He has remained by my side always! GLORRRRRYYYY!! Give God the ultimate Praise for what He has ALREADY done in your life!! YOUR VICTORY IS IN YOUR MOUTH! YOUR VICTORY IS IN YOUR PRAISE! I pray blessings upon you!!

As I prayed this morning,

I was thinking, I could've been dead! I could've lost my mind! I could've been an uncaring parent! I could've been a drug addict! I could've been an alcoholic! I could've been so many things that are looked down upon, but God had another plan for my life!!

So, the next time you EVEN THINK ABOUT COMPLAINING, GETTING UPSET, or even WORRYING about your current situation; think about where you COULD HAVE been in your life right now! That's enough to make you want to SHOUT AND PRAISE HIM RIGHT THERE!! I'm singing, "YOUR GRACE AND M-ER-C-Y!! BROUGHT ME THROUGH! I'M LIVING THIS MO-M-E-N-T BECAUSE OF YOU! I WANT TO THANK YOU AND PRAISE YOU TOO!! YOUR G-R-A-C-E AND M-E-R-C-Y, BROUGHT ME THROUGH!!"

LS

ANGER

What word would you use to describe these scenarios??

"Oh, I know he didn't just hit my brand-new car, I'm about to go off on that old man!!"

"These children are getting on my last nerve, they are going to make me hurt them!"

"So how did he get a pay raise and I didn't!??!!"

"So she's talking about me behind my #$%^& back??!! Oh, I'll fix that!"

What word would you use to describe these scenarios??...**ANGER**. Evan Esar said, "Anger is a feeling that makes your mouth work faster than your mind." I agree...situations arise, people say or do something and our emotions take over quickly! We go around saying we are having a bad day because a certain person/situation made us angry. How dare we let a person/situation dictate our day!

No one can do no more than you allow them to do. Don't allow anger to stress you out! While you're still angry, the other person has moved on and they're having a good day. We all deal with anger from time-to- time, but what matters is how you handle it. Read and re-read Ephesians 4:26, "Be ye angry, and sin not: let not the sun go down upon your wrath: Neither give place to the devil." Don't give the devil opportunity to step in and take over! Do what God called you to do. So instead of being bitter, get better! Overcome anger by praying for those or the situation that hurt you. It may seem hard to do at first, but stay with it and allow God to take you through the process! I pray blessings upon you!

Maximize this moment …

The moment you realize that you have to go through something if you want to get to something, and you are ready to go through and get it!

BE ENCOURAGED

I don't care what you have done....

As long as you are alive, there is hope for you! Don't allow the enemy to convince you that all hope is lost! The fact that you're still alive is an indication that GOD is working with you! God is GREATER than EVERYTHING that has EVER come against you! I pray blessings upon you! Much Love!

DON'T LET ANYONE OR ANYTHING STEAL YOUR JOY! When life seems to be leading you astray and that black cloud of despair is just hovering over you. Stop everything you are doing, turn off any distractions! Start worshiping God and do not stop until you get lost in His presence!! Psalm 16:11 says, "Thou wilt show me the path of life: in your presence is the fullness of joy; at thy right hand are pleasures for evermore."

I remember this saying: "DON'T BE OVERWHELMED WITH MY DAY, BE OVERWHELMED WITH MY GOD!" God is always there for you! Even when you think he's not, He is right there! GLORY!! HALLELUJAH!! Singing..."I get JOY when I think about what He's done for me!! I get JOY when I think about what He's done for me!!" LIVE YOUR LIFE IN FULL EXPECTATION THAT SOMETHING GREAT IS ALWAYS HAPPENING TO YOU AND FOR YOU! I pray blessings upon you! Much Love!

When the world says No, "BUT GOD" says YES! The world says You can't, "BUT GOD" says YOU CAN! The world says, Don't, "BUT GOD" says, DO! The world says Won't, "But God" says WILL! Ephesians 2:4-6 "But God, who is rich in mercy, for his great love wherewith he loved us, even when we were dead in sins, hath quickened us together with Christ, and hath raised us up together, and made us sit together in heavenly places in Christ Jesus!" I pray blessings upon you!!

I want to encourage you……don't move, don't jump, don't quit, STAND RIGHT THERE! If you can make it through, EVERYTHING God promised you will show up in the place of your cry unto God! Show me the place of your greatest weakness and I'll show you the place of your greatest strength! Show me the place that broke you and I'll show you the place of your greatest comeback! I pray blessings upon you! Much Love!

BLESSINGS

BE ENCOURAGED BY THE BLESSINGS ABOUT TO TAKE PLACE IN YOUR FUTURE! CLAIM THEM AND KEEP TELLING YOURSELF HOW BLESSED YOU ARE. TAPE IT TO THE WALL. MAKE A POSTER BOARD. WRITE IT ON A T-SHIRT. WHATEVER YOU NEED TO DO TO KEEP YOUR EYES ON THE PRIZE, DO IT! "THE PAST IS THE PAST!" YOUR NEGATIVE PAST DOES NOT DETERMINE YOUR INCREDIBLE FUTURE! I PRAY BLESSINGS UPON YOU! MUCH LOVE!

"If you fall down seven times get up eight!" Remember that Paul tells us in Philippians 3:13 that he tries to forget what's behind him and reach forward to what's ahead. Reach forward to those things God has prepared for you! I use to think that when I failed in life, I was a failure as a person but I can tell you this, that couldn't have been further from the truth.
NEVER allow those failures and negative past situations to "imprison you!"

If you apply for a job seven times, go apply for the eighth one! If you tried to stop smoking seven times, try an 8th time! If you tried to start a business seven times, go the 8th round! Get the picture? Don't allow yourself to be '"shut-up", or "shut down" in a dungeon of failure! Don't relive those past failures over and over again! YOU ARE A CHILD OF GOD! GO DO IT AGAIN, AND AGAIN, AND IT WILL HAPPEN! Faith comes by hearing and victory comes by faith, believing that you can and not giving up. I pray blessings upon you!!

STAY ENCOURAGED!!! God has a way of TURNING the worst situation into the GREATEST blessing we ever imagined! WHATEVER the path God sends you down, know that He has already equipped you for the journey (mentally, physically and spiritually)! Even though the way may not be smooth; He will never give you more than you can bear! Now think on this; when you're going through "trying" times and you want to give up and quit, why would you quit? You would just have to go through the drudgery of starting all over again! Don't let ANYBODY tell you that you can't do something that's in the Will of God! The bible says you can do ALL THINGS THROUGH CHRIST WHO STRENGTHENS YOU! If God said IT, BELIEVE IT and let that SETTLE IT! I continue to say....BE ENCOURAGED! IT "AIN'T" OVER, UNTIL GOD SAYS IT'S OVER! I pray blessings upon you! Much Love!

God, I thank you right now for your many

blessings. I pray that others are filled with your MIGHTY GLORIOUS STRENGTH so they can keep going....no matter what! Our Strength comes from YOU! Wrap your loving arms around those who are hurting, in pain, depressed, lonely, and suicidal, worrying, angry, and doubtful! Help them to walk in YOUR LIGHT and may YOUR LOVE bless them!

Jeremiah 29:11 says, "For I know the plans I have for you," declares the Lord, "plans to prosper you and not to harm you, plans to give you hope and a future. I pray this in JESUS NAME!! AMEN!!

BREAK DOWN WALLS

BREAK DOWN THOSE WALLS!! Walls of depression, Walls of destruction, Walls of doubt, Walls of fear, Walls of worry, Walls of sickness, Walls of discouragement, Walls of low self-esteem. BREAK DOWN THOSE WALLS! WHY? BECAUSE GOD IS TAKING YOU UP AND OVER WALLS THAT HAVE HELD YOU IN AND KEPT YOU OUT! CLAIM IT! BELIEVE IT AND RECEIVE IT! I PRAY BLESSINGS UPON YOU!

God is in the business of breaking down walls. Take hope! Take heart! This too will pass. The truth will come forth and make you free. Every day walls of depression come down, walls of stress come down, walls of financial struggle come down, walls of sickness come down, and walls of tribulation come down! Don't focus on the trials and tribulations…….. God will take care of the bad things in your life, because God is helping you to breakthrough those walls that have held you in! BREAKTHROUGH the walls….

"GOD I'M CLAIMING MY COMPLETE BREAKTHROUGH of EVERY WALL IN MY LIFE!" THE REST OF MY DAYS WILL BE THE BEST OF MY DAYS!!!!

CHALLENGE

Challenge: a calling into question, a demanding of proof, explanation, a call or dare to take part in or be a part of something. I CHALLENGE you, take this challenge, and meet this CHALLENGE!

I CHALLENGE you to Live in your today and do those things that are necessary for today that make for a better and brighter tomorrow.

I CHALLENGE you to do better, to be better, to think, to grow, to give, to live! I challenge you to improve your mind, to improve your quality of life, to develop your gifts, and serve God.
  I CHALLENGE you to become, to go get, to rise up, and to overcome!

I challenge you to think of someone other than yourself, pray for other than yourself, help other than yourself, get involved with projects other than your own!

I CHALLENGE you to Plan for tomorrow, see where you are and yet keep pointing to where you want to be. I CHALLENGE you to Walk away from yesterday, learn from the lessons of a painful yesterday, forgive and walk away, and do not sabotage your future by bringing the thought patterns of the painful experiences with you. Loose the hurt and move forward!

CHAOS

Can you praise God in the middle of CHAOS? God knows you're hurting! He knows all about what is in your life and what's going on around you. Know that God is in control of it ALL! My soul can be still in the midst of chaos, storms, and confusion because I know God is on MY side and He is the author and finisher of my faith! He has faithfully led me in the past and I KNOW He will continue to guide my path in the future!

You don't need to ask God to move the chaos but ask God to CALM you in the middle of it all!

I thank God for the ability to pray and remain faithful while going through in the midst of chaos! Isaiah 41:10 says, "Fear not, for I am with you; Be not dismayed, for I am your God. I will strengthen you, Yes, I will help you, I will uphold you with My righteous right hand." NOW PRAISE HIM while you're going through! Our PRAISE will bring the PEACE! Don't let the chaos take you over on today! PRAISE HIM IN THE MIDDLE OF THE CHAOS!! GLORY!!

Chaos is the lack of order. Many people look at their lives and see things in order and take for granted that it will always be that way. God help us to remember that every day is precious and that nothing should be taken for granted! Give us the strength to keep fighting when we feel like disorder is taking over our lives! As we face today's journey, I pray that you turn every obstacle into an opportunity! God, only you know why we go through the things we do! Thank you for helping us to move beyond things that are out of order, and for allowing us to see opportunities during our chaos!

IT DOESN'T MATTER HOW MANY TIMES I GET DISORGANIZED AND OFF TRACK, YOU TAUGHT ME HOW TO GET IT BACK TOGETHER, KEEP MY HEAD UP AND KEEP WALKING BY FAITH!! When I think about all the times when things in my life have been off course...and how You spoke to Chaos and said LET THERE BE ORDER! I SHOUT AND I PRAISE YOUR NAME!!!

Maximize this moment …

The moment you began to believe God is about to turn things around for you! I don't care what it looks like; Stay in FAITH, and SPEAK LIFE!!

DON'T QUIT

"I REFUSE TO QUIT!" Don't put your Faith in people, but put it in God! We have all gone through some disappointments from time-to-time. Disappointments reveal our character, and how we handle them lets us know who we really are! When you are ready to give up on life, God isn't ready to give up on you! Every time you've gone through something, God did, or He was and remains, ready to see you through?? This time is no different, He's the same God yesterday, today and forever!! You don't get "developed" when things are easy and bright! You get developed in the dark room of life. God is developing you during the tough times! If you want to know the outcome of your blessings, look at the weight of your burdens!! Hallelujah! Be the PICTURE of perseverance and say with me, "I REFUSE TO QUIT!" I pray blessings upon you!

W HAT! I hear you say, "I'm tired, I'm going to QUIT, I can't take it anymore! WAIT!! I AM here to tell you that, NO WEAPON FORMED AGAINST YOU SHALL PROSPER!" When you speak those words in FAITH and BELIEVE them as TRUTH, those things you are up against cannot win over YOU! You don't have to become stressed out about the negative words or actions that are thrown your way! Put your FAITH in what God has promised YOU!!! Let me say that again, put your FAITH in what God has promised YOU! Every tongue that rises against you, you will put to shame and make their words inaccurate and obsolete. You can't quit now, your blessing is only a prayer, praise, a proclamation, and a person away!

Y ou've survived and made it this far! You will make it farther! Stop stressing over things you can't change. Philippians 4:6-7 "Be worried for nothing, but in everything by prayer and supplication, with thanksgiving, let your requests be made known to God; and the peace of God, which surpasses all understanding, will guard your hearts and minds through Christ Jesus." Refuse to allow your circumstances to dictate how you're going to feel! You choose how you want to feel in this moment. COMMAND your feelings and determine to have a victorious attitude because YOU ARE A WINNER! STAY FOCUSED AND KNOW THAT GOD WILL PROVIDE AND GIVE YOU STRENGTH TO MAKE IT! ENJOY YOUR LIFE AND MAXIMIZE YOUR MOMENTS! I pray blessings upon you!

There are times when we do get TIRED and EXHAUSTED but you can't QUIT! Oh, no, I AM here to tell you that you can't QUIT! You were declared a WINNER long before the race even STARTED! God created you to OVERCOME AND conquer! So, there's no way you can continue to feel and tell yourself you are losing! It may look like you're losing, but it always appears the hero is losing, but in the end, the hero always comes out on top! So, look up because that's where you are headed, UP! I pray blessings upon you!

Think on this……Anyone can give up; it's the easiest thing in the world to do! But to actually hold it TOGETHER when everyone else you know has fallen apart and would understand if you fell apart, NOW THAT'S TRUE STRENGTH! God, I thank you for the STRENGTH that has developed in ME! Repeat that statement and add your name! CLAIM IT RIGHT NOW!! I pray an abundance of blessings upon you!!

GIVE IT ALL TO GOD!! Even when people want to tell you negative things about your situation(s). Don't Settle For That! YOU ARE UNIQUE, YOU ARE SPECIAL, YOU ARE A CHILD OF GOD, YOU DO MAKE A DIFFERENCE IN THIS LIFE……WHY? BECAUSE YOU DON'T HAVE TO SETTLE!! SOMETIMES IT MAY TAKE SOME PATIENCE AND WAITING....BUT NEVER FORGET....GOD GOT THIS!!

Maximize this moment ...

The moment you realize a change is about to take place in your life! GIVE GOD THE GLORY AND THE PRAISE FOR IT RIGHT NOW!!!

FAITH

Start praising God, like you've already got it!!!

"FAITH" it, to you make it!! Don't let fear and doubt put hands on your FAITH!! "FAITH, FAITH, FAITH, MUSTARD SEED FAITH, YOU DON'T NEED A WHOLE LOT, JUST USE THE LITTLE YOU GOT AND WATCH MOUNTAINS MOVE OUT OF YOUR WAY!" I PRAY BLESSINGS UPON YOU! MUCH LOVE

FAMILY

If we don't PRAY for our children the devil will PREY on our children! Anoint them as they sleep, sow love, patience, and education into them! No matter how far away they seem at times, keep believing God for their breakthrough! Don't give up on them and tell them about God, because a godless generation will destroy themselves.

If you have family that you are not speaking to, please make amends with them today. It breaks my heart to hear people "bashing" their family. Every day, especially the holidays, are always difficult for me because I lost both my parents as a child (missing them terribly) ...and growing up with no siblings made it harder. Love your family unconditionally! They make mistakes just like you do.... forgive, love them, move on, pray for one another, share, extend a hand, give your heart, be a blessing! Forgive and allow God to handle the rest!

LS

FORGIVENESS

Is it hard for you to forgive someone? Have we forgotten this POWERFUL scripture in the Bible? Matthew 6:14-15, "For if ye forgive men their trespasses, your Heavenly Father will also forgive you; but if you forgive not men their trespasses, neither will your Father forgive your trespasses." If we allow the root of bitterness to spring up in our hearts against someone, our prayers will be hindered. I had a hard time dealing with "forgiveness" many years ago. I allowed the hurt and pain to live in my heart for years. Then I wondered why I wasn't growing spiritually? God said to me, when you release that bitterness, anger, pain, hurt, resentment, you will experience such a PEACE! I thank God for deliverance, after that I began to grow. In this moment you can receive a forgiving heart and mind which will open the doors of your life to a brighter day! An abundance of blessings to you!

Maximize this moment ...

The moment you began to believe that your mouth speaks forth the mind of God for the purpose of your life, and SPEAK it!!

God

What the enemy meant for evil, GOD will turn for your good! Yes... the enemy comes to kill, steal and destroy but ONLY if you let him! Don't let the "Distracter", distract you! Whatever the enemy INTENDED to do, God can turn that AROUND if you turn to HIM! Turn to the Word of God…. Romans 8:28 says, "And we know that all things work together for good to them that love God, to them who are the called according to His purpose." God will not leave you or forsake you in the midst of your trial if you focus on Him! I pray blessings upon you!

God will not ask you to do anything today that will not make you stronger for tomorrow! Meditate on this Word: Proverbs 3:5-6 "Trust in the LORD with all your heart; and lean not unto your own understanding. In all thy ways acknowledge him, and he shall direct your path." Ask God what to do today and let Him lead you through. I pray blessings upon you and prosperity!

Our God is a Restorer! It is not done until God says it's done! He is a God of Restoration...life restored, family restored, heath restored, job restored. You don't have to try to fix the problem on your own! Let it go and let God in, He will RESTORE what you have lost! I pray blessings upon you!

God is STRONGER than any PROBLEM that you face! Instead of speaking negative and worrying about your situation...take the time to pray, "Lord, I'm going through hard times right now, AND IN THE MIDST OF IT ALL... I THANK YOU for what YOU are going to do for me!! Don't let me ever turn away from YOU, no matter how many trials and difficulties I face! Let these difficulties serve to make me stronger and sincerer to YOU!" Here's a saying that I heard a long time ago: "DON'T TELL GOD THAT YOU HAVE A BIG PROBLEM, TELL YOUR PROBLEM THAT YOU HAVE A BIG GOD!!"

God is in control ALWAYS! When you "know" and "believe" that, you can say the following: "STRESS DOESN'T LIVE HERE ANYMORE!" "FEAR NEEDS TO GO BACK WHERE IT CAME FROM!" "DEPRESSION IS NOT TAKING OVER MY MIND!" "SICKNESS WILL NOT TAKE OVER MY BODY!" I AM ON GOD'S SIDE AND HE HAS IT ALL UNDER CONTROL, I WILL NOT FEAR, FRET, OR FALTER BUT I WILL PRAISE BECAUSE MY GOD IS IN CONTROL! I PRAY BLESSINGS UPON YOU!

God will NEVER put more on you than you can bear!! Never forget that God is our "Burden Bearer!" The strength of God comes in and becomes everything you need and more! Read the lyrics of this following song: "I've gone through the fire and I've been through the flood. I've been broken into pieces and seen lightning' flashing' from above. But through it all, I remember...That He loves me.... And He cares.... And He'll never put more on me than I can bear!!"

NO, YOU ARE NOT ALONE, GOD IS WITH YOU! STAND and believe GOD, casting your care upon Him because He cares for YOU! I pray blessings upon you! Much love!

God says, "The reason why you can't see the door I just opened...is because you are still staring at the window I just closed." God says, "I want to fix it for you, but you keep getting in the way and trying to fix it yourself." God says, "I know you need a financial breakthrough, don't speak negatively It's on the way." Believe God and believe that He is working behind the scenes: moving some things, establishing some things, creating, designing and putting some things in order just for YOU! Don't give up now, ONLY BELIEVE AND RECEIVE THE PROMISES OF GOD!!! I pray blessings upon you! Much love!

NEVER let a bad situation bring out the bad in you! What is meant for evil, God will use for good! Situations may hurt you, but NEVER, EVER let them break you! Sometimes you must say a prayer, "God, I may not understand why everything is happening in my life right now, but I trust YOU and I love YOU!

AMEN!!" You just put it in God's hands, now look up and let GOD FIGHT, because the BATTLE is not yours, it's the LORD's! I pray blessings upon you!

GOD IS GREATER than those bills! GOD IS GREATER than that sickness! GOD IS GREATER than that job you lost! GOD IS GREATER than any enemy! GOD IS GREATER than that foreclosure! GOD IS GREATER than that depression! GOD IS GREATER! Look at your situation and say, "This situation may look bad RIGHT NOW, but I KNOW GOD is in the midst of it all!!" Sometimes you may...feel like God is sooooooo quiet....and that he is not making any NOISE concerning your situation......but let me tell you, GOD is speaking PEACE to your situation! 1 John 3:20 says, "For if our heart condemns us, God is greater than our heart, and knoweth all things." Trust that God is working on your behalf!! HE'S writing you a letter: "To Whom it may Concern, I Am God and I AM WORKING THIS OUT FOR YOU!"

GRATEFUL

BE GRATEFUL EVERYDAY!! Always THANK GOD for what YOU do have instead of what YOU don't have! When we have everything we need, we tend to be happy and joyful.... but the minute we are without something, we want to let doubt, worry and fear overtake our mind. Didn't the Word of God say: "Therefore I say unto you, take no thought for your life, what ye shall eat, or what ye shall drink; nor yet for your body, what ye shall put on. Is not the life more than meat, and the body than clothes?" Embrace this powerful Word of God! THANK GOD FOR WHAT YOU HAVE AND TRUST GOD FOR WHAT YOU NEED! AGAIN, THANK GOD FOR WHAT YOU HAVE AND TRUST GOD FOR WHAT YOU NEED!! I pray blessings upon you! Much love!

Maximize this moment ...

The moment you move in Peace! Bless someone else in this moment! Give someone a smile in this moment! Forgive your enemies in this moment! Tell someone you love them in this moment and mean it as you MAXIMIZE THIS MOMENT!

HEALING

Thank God for your Grace and Mercy! The doctors gave you one report, but God has a better report for you. "Whose report are you going to believe?" Believe God for your complete healing right now! He is a healer and the Most High God! You give us LIFE and the gift of infinite JOY! You hold all power in your hands! In YOU all things are possible! YOU hold our heart within YOURS! Say this affirmation: Thank You God for YOUR healing LIFE that surges throughout every cell of my entire being... strengthening me and restoring me to wholeness! My Faith is not wavered, shaken, nor in doubt! I speak, claim, believe, and receive my blessing as I draw strength from YOU! I place my confidence and trust in YOU! I speak this in the Mighty Name of JESUS!

Psalm 16:8 says, "I have set the LORD always before me: because he is at my right hand, I shall not be moved." "I WILL NOT BE SHAKEN!"

Ok, now tell YOURSELF, "I WILL NOT BE SHAKEN!"
Tell sickness, "I will NOT be shaken!"
Tell pain, "I will NOT be shaken!"
Tell the enemy, "I will NOT be shaken!"
Tell depression, "I will NOT be shaken!"
Tell fear, "I will NOT be shaken!"
Tell poverty, "I will NOT be shaken!"
Tell doubt, "I will NOT be shaken!"
Ok, now tell YOURSELF again, "I WILL NOT BE SHAKEN!"

LS

I feel a need in my spirit to say this...on the week I received that devastating report from the doctor of having Lupus, immediately it tore me up inside. I said, "God I'm going through enough already, why more?" Then I asked that million-dollar question, "Why me Lord?" Well, we know that answer...."Why not you. I know you can handle it." I prayed and cried out to God! I had to change my way of thinking from the day before..."I'm a strong woman, this is another journey I have to go through and I will make it!" "I'm a conqueror!" "I'm HEALED!" "I will NOT hang my head down!" "I'm tired, but GOD will give me strength!" Just hold on..."I WILL have a mighty testimony one day!" Not for my benefit, but to help someone else and to give God ALL the GLORY and ALL the PRAISE! I'm claiming it RIGHT NOW!! In the NAME of JESUS!! I have too much work to do for God!

Maximize this moment...

Hold your head up! A change is about to take place in your life! Give God the glory and believe it NOW!

HOLD YOUR HEAD UP

Hey! Yes, I'm talking to you! Is your head hanging down? If so why? Hold it up high! Stand up straight! Look that trouble, problem, circumstance, enemy, pain, depression, heartache, trouble in the EYES!!

SPEAK VICTORY FOR YOUR LIFE INTO EXISTENCE RIGHT NOW!! DON'T JUST SAY IT, BELIEVE IT! Repeat after me: "NOTHING CAN HOLD ME DOWN!" "NO WEAPON FORMED AGAINST ME SHALL PROSPER!" "I'M A CHILD OF GOD!" "I'M BLESSED AND HIGHLY FAVORED!" "I GOT KNOCKED DOWN, BUT I'M GETTING BACK UP AGAIN!" "THE LORD IS MY SHEPHERD I SHALL NOT WANT!" "MY GOD IS ABLE TO SEE ME THROUGH ANY CIRCUMSTANCE!" "I'M TOO BLESSED TO BE STRESSED!" HALLELUJAH!!!! NOW WALK INTO YOUR DELIVERANCE!!! GLORY!! WILL YOURSELF TO FEEL GOOD RIGHT NOW!! I PRAY BLESSINGS UPON YOUR LIFE! MUCH LOVE!!

Are you feeling down today? If so, YOU might as well hold YOUR head up, and look toward the hills from whence cometh YOUR help....and say, "MY HELP COMES FROM THE LORD!" Matthew 11:28 says, " Come unto me, all ye that labor and are heavy laden, and I will give you rest. Take my yoke upon you, and learn of me; for I am meek and lowly in heart: and ye shall find rest unto your souls. YOU might as well hold YOUR head up because after you have gotten to the bottom, the only place to go is up! I pray blessings upon your life!

HOLD YOUR HEAD UP! We all make mistakes and not everything that we try is going to be successful. If you give up after a couple of setbacks, you'll never make it, but if you keep trying a change will come! DON'T GIVE UP! DON'T QUIT! DON'T GIVE UP! DON'T QUIT! DON'T GIVE UP! DON'T QUIT! CAN YOU HEAR ME NOW? LET GO OF SETBACKS AND LIVE! I pray blessings upon your life!

There is a song that says, "No matter what, you're going through... Remember God is using you, For the battle is not yours, it's the Lord's!" WHATEVER you're going through on THIS DAY, stay strong and go through it because this battle is NOT yours!! Singing...."No matter what it is that you're going through...Hold your head up, stick your chest out...and remember, He's bringing you out of what you're going through." God is going to bring you through! "GLORY!!! NO DEPRESSION, WORRY, STRESS, OR HEARTACHE IS BIGGER THAN OUR GOD!! THE BATTLE IS NOT YOURS! IT'S THE LORD'S! I PRAY BLESSINGS UPON YOUR LIFE!

The same people who sat at the table and JUDGED you, are the same ones who are about to see you walk in total VICTORY!! Don't give up because someone said you can't do something, instead let that motivate you to move forward! Hold your head up high, grit your teeth, and STAND! Don't stress over anything you can't control, because while you're trying to figure it out, God has already worked it out! GLORY! No weapon formed against you shall prosper, and if God is for you, He is MORE than anything that comes against you!! I pray blessings upon your life!

LS

Maximize this moment...

The moment you realize that at the heart of every storm is VICTORY waiting to be claimed!!! Claim it and create a beautiful and blessed you in this moment!!

LETTING GO!!

Give it all over to God! Psalm 55:22

"Cast your burden on the Lord, And He shall sustain you; He shall never permit the righteous to be moved." Have PEACE, BELIEVE God, CLAIM IT, and RECEIVE IT!! It's now time for God's people to bury anything that has been dragging you down, making you bitter, holding you back, limiting your skills, keeping you depressed, and taking away your joy. Put it all in a coffin, allow it to be lowered into the ground and have FAITH and BELIEVE it's OVER in your life! Don't reach in the coffin to get any of those things! LET IT GO! LET IT GO! Once it's buried, don't try to "dig" it back up! It is marked DNR-Do Not Resuscitate! LET IT GO AND MOVE FORWARD! You can do it! I pray blessings upon your life!

Why don't you file for divorce? Lisa did that a long time ago! Today! Divorce your past, divorce your failures, divorce depression, divorce doubt, divorce any setbacks, divorce dead-end relationships, divorce pain, divorce bitterness, divorce jealousy, divorce insecurities and divorce the lack of spending time with God! Rid your life of those things that produce failure and setback in your life. Get rid of them! You mean to tell me you are happy with hanging on to the same things that let you down? Leave all that baggage behind in the divorce! You now stand before "The

Judge", and God the just judge, has granted you an uncontested divorce from your past. In this verdict you also have been given FULL CUSTODY of your inheritance, FULL CUSTODY of your destiny, and FULL CUSTODY of your purpose in life! You now have that "Stamp of Approval!" PRAISE HIM, BECAUSE YOU ARE FREE!! STEP OUT ON FAITH! GLORY!! CLAIM IT, BELIEVE IT, AND RECEIVE IT! I pray blessings upon your life! Much Love!

If you hold onto your past, your hands aren't open to the FUTURE that GOD has for you! Let go of what use to be and allow GOD's will to be done! Let go and allow GOD to move out the old and bring in the NEW! I pray blessings upon your life!

Repeat after me: TODAY.... I am going to let my burdens go! I am going to face this day and have Faith that everything WILL get better!! God, you WILL provide for my every need, in every way! I'm staying focused!!! Staying motivated, inspired, encouraged, driven, energized, empowered, and BLESSED!!!!

.

LS

LOW SELF-ESTEEM

Man to Woman: "No man is going to want you with four kids! You're fat and you only have a high school education!"

Wife to Husband: "You are just worthless! That's all the money you made on your job? How are we going to make it? I need a man with a better job!"

Mother to Son: "Your grades are terrible! You are not going to amount to anything! With your dumb @%#!"

Classmate to Classmate: "You wear hand-me down clothes every day and you're ugly too!"

Being told these harmful words over and over again can bring about LOW SELF-ESTEEM. Have you experienced things in your life that brought your self-worth and esteem down? If Satan can rob us of our self-esteem, then he can hinder us from accomplishing the works of God. Satan's job is to convince us that our efforts are worthless, that we don't matter, and everything we've accomplished is no good and hopeless.

Instead of dwelling on Satan's "down-grades," let's improve, and get a heavenly UPGRADE! True self-esteem comes from God: "I can do all things through Christ which strengthens me." Be affirmed by the promises of God. "My grace is sufficient for thee: for my strength is made perfect in weakness." Don't let negative things take you down and break you down until you become broken-down. STAND-UP, be LIFTED-UP and REJOICE-UP for what God is doing in your life! Think on positive things as an important part of what goes into making you complete. We need good self-worth and positive esteem, therefore adopt an "I CAN" attitude. Eliminate negative self-talk from your vocabulary and don't receive garbage from others. Your life has a purpose and you can be anything God enables you to be! BE ENCOURAGED AND STAY ENCOURAGED! I pray blessings upon your life!

Maximize this moment ...

The moment you feel a break-through about to happen in your life right now!! Go ahead and CLAIM IT and thank GOD for IT as you MAXIMIZE THIS MOMENT!

MIRACLES

I don't care what the devil has told you!! You ARE next up for a MIRACLE, CLAIM IT! Don't give up!! Your MIRACLE is on the way! JUST BELIEVE!! When you completely trust God, you don't have to wonder if you're going to make it through ...JUST KNOW IT! JUST BELIEVE IT! God has a MIRACLE coming for you!
I pray blessings upon your life!

Your miracle is a person away, THERE'S A MAN LOOKING FOR YOU! There's a person set up and sent by God to change the trajectory of your life to implement a new thing that He wants to do in you and with you! JUST KNOW IT! JUST BELIEVE IT! God has a MIRACLE coming for you!

NEGATIVITY

Don't allow NEGATIVE people to determine your day, your week, or your life. Negative + Negative = Negative! It may seem like no matter what you do, someone has something negative to say about you and find fault....so what do you do? Matthew 5:11-12 says, "Blessed are you when they insult and single you out, and say all kinds of evil against you falsely on My behalf. Rejoice and be exceedingly glad, for great is your reward in heaven, for so they persecuted the prophets who were before you." One thing you should do is LOVE yourself, yes that's right...LOVE YOURSELF! When you love yourself, you are secure with who you are. Then you don't place attention into the negative things others say against you, because where attention goes power flows. Instead, YOU will control your power and manifest what GOD has put inside of YOU!

The best thing you can do when you cannot find a place of agreement with a negative person is praying for them and leave them alone! Keep a POSITIVE mind and know YOUR OWN PURPOSE! I pray blessings upon your life!

NO WEAPON FORMED AGAINST YOU

We can let what we are going through today either MAKE US or BREAK US! There is ABSOLUTELY NOTHING you can go through today that you and God together can't get through! Psalm 46:1 says, "God is our refuge and strength, a very present help in trouble." STAY ENCOURAGED this too will pass!! I pray blessings upon your life!

When people hurt you, God will be there to heal you! When people humiliate you, God will magnify you! When people judge you, God will justify you!

Isaiah 54:17 says, "NO WEAPON FORMED AGAINST ME SHALL PROSPER!" When we speak those words in Faith and believe them as Truth, those who are against you NEVER win, even if it appears they are ahead, they will never defeat you. You don't have to become stressed out about the negative words or actions that are thrown your way!

Every tongue that speaks against you, YOU will destroy and bring their words down to the ground. Give your enemies no ammunition to triumph over you and when they rise up to bring accusations, turn to God and let HIS grace and mercy prevail in your time of testing. I pray blessings upon your life! Much Love!

"No Weapon formed against me shall prosper! It won't work!" Do you walk in favor? No! YOU walk in AWESOME FAVOR! Because the favor of God is amazingly AWESOME, therefore YOU are blessed, HEALED, DELIVERED, and VICTORIOUS! Remember there is power in your words, so SPEAK LIFE today, speak blessings, speak Favor don't just speak it but BELIEVE IT. YOU were giving the power to set the tone of your day, not someone else! If someone or "something" tries to shake you up today, just start singing aloud or quietly, "NO WEAPON, FORMED AGAINST ME, SHALL PROSPER! IT WON'T WORK!!" Then just step back out of the way and watch God work!! GLORY TO GOD FOR THE GREAT THINGS HE HAS DONE AND WILL DO IN YOUR LIFE! I pray blessings upon your life!

"No Weapon formed against me shall prosper! It won't work!" I walk in awesome favor.........YOU walk in awesome favor! I'm blessed! YOU are blessed! I am HEALED! YOU are HEALED! Remember there is power in your words, so SPEAK LIFE today, speak blessings, and speak Favor... but don't just speak it, but BELIEVE IT! YOU were given the power to set the tone of your day, not someone else! If someone or "something" tries to shake you up today, just start singing, "NO WEAPON, FORMED AGAINST ME, SHALL PROSPER! IT WON'T WORK!!" Then just step back out of the way and watch God work!!

LS

Maximize this moment ...

The moment you find a way to win, even when it seems you are losing. Victory is yours!!

OPPORTUNITY

Each day you wake up in the morning and you smell God's good air, ITS ANOTHER OPPORTUNITY. Opportunities to change a life, change a community, change a city, change a nation, or even change a world. Don't waste it by procrastinating. Don't miss it by being distracted by things that don't matter. Don't ignore it by being indifferent with a casual attitude about your daily routine and most important, don't take it for granted by having an ungrateful attitude toward the good things you have that some may never know! One of the greatest gifts God has given you is the power to take full advantage of an opportunity. You're waiting for God to make everything in your life right but God is excited about you moving forward creatively with the opportunity. The opportunity is your blessing that will open the windows of heaven that there won't be room enough to receive, GLORY!! I pray blessings upon your life!

If God shuts a door, stop banging on it! Trust that whatever is behind it is not meant for you! God closes doors so that you can change directions. Closed doors in your life are God's way of getting your attention! Thank God for them! He is pointing you to a new direction in life for new OPPORTUNITIES. "In God's own time, He will bring you through it and to it!" God closes doors so that you will find HIS open door! Be ready and stay ready for the GREAT OPPORTUNITIES that God has kept in store just for YOU! I pray blessings upon your life!

Some doors are meant to be closed, therefore leave them closed! Your blessing is not behind anything that is closed up and "used to be." STAY Encouraged! God has something new and exciting for you behind new doors with fresh OPPORTUNITIES. He will lead you to the right door and hold it open for you and no one will go in and get what's yours but YOU! Your blessing is not late; God has PERFECT TIMING! GLORY!

<u>PICK YOUR BATTLES</u>

In this life, you must pick your battles that are worth your time, energy, purpose, and other resources. Think about it, is it that important to you to have the "last word", when actions speak louder?   Do you really have to prove people wrong, for no gain at all? When something negative happens to someone, do you really have to say, "See, I told you so!" Our "Ego" can be a hindrance to our success! Let's try "Silence" with positive and effective action. It will be louder and more powerful than any word you ever speak! Proverbs 11:12 says, "... a person of shrewdness and wisdom power maintains their peace." I pray blessings upon your life!

LS

PRAYER

God wants to use you to pray the prayer of supplication for others. I want to encourage you to begin to pray for others and expect God to answer! Philippians 4:6-7 "Be worried for nothing, but in everything by prayer and petition, with thanksgiving make your requests known to God; and the peace of God, which exceeds all understanding, will guard your hearts and minds through Christ Jesus." Remember God determined, knows, and sees the big picture unfolding. So if the answer is not what you expect, don't feel your prayer went unanswered. He just might have something bigger and better coming! "Supplication is the prayer that moves in the confidence of the peace we have that God is or has worked it out for us and the ones we are praying for." Let's pray for one another! "The effectual fervent prayer of a righteous man avails much." Bless someone else TODAY as I pray blessings upon your life!

The BEST way to STOP worrying is to START praying!! PRAYER changes things and prayer changes the attitude and perspective of the one praying! What does worry change? NOTHING! John 14:27 says, "Peace I leave with you, my real, uncontaminated, fulfilling peace I give unto you, but I give it not according to the world's system of giving." Do not allow your heart to be troubled, neither allow it to be afraid." Worrying is the opposite of TRUSTING GOD!! REMEMBER, JEHOVAH JIREH, MY GOD WILL PROVIDE!! God Knows and Will Meet Your Every Need! GLORY!! I pray blessings upon your life!

See: **MY PRAYERS OF MOTIVATION TO GET YOU THROUGH THE ROUGH PLACES**

Maximize this moment ...

The moment they were hoping you would fall but you fell forward,
got up, stayed up, prayed up, and went further than they thought you would go!

RELATIONSHIP

If you can't be patient, content & happy when you are "single," then more than likely you won't be happy, content or patient when married. No person should be made to feel responsible for your happiness because at some point they will falter and fail to meet your expectations. Mature in your single state and become complete within yourself so that God can bless you to have a fruitful, happy, and successful marriage.

STORMS and SETBACKS

Think about for a moment how many storms and setbacks you've endured in your lifespan. Now think about this... You are STILL HERE! Which means, "YOU MADE IT THROUGH!" GLORY!! So, the next time you encounter adversity, remember that you made it through other storms, so believe by God and your victories that you can make it through this also!

I want you to know that no matter HOW MUCH you had to overcome and still may have to overcome, your story is not over because there is still MORE GLORY IN YOUR STORY! Have faith in your ability to overcome anything put in your way! I pray blessings upon your life!

If a "storm" is going on all around you, know that you are in a perfect position for God to STRENGTHEN you so that you can do more than just endure the storm, but YOU CAN OVERCOME it! A scripture that I carry within is Psalm 46:1 "God is our refuge and strength, a very present help in trouble." Never Doubt the Mighty Work of GOD, even while in the midst of a storm you are still more than a conqueror! Someone YOU know needs to hear this on today! I pray blessings upon your life!

STRESS

Lisa is TOO BLESSED TOO BE STRESSED!! If you are stressed on today, write a letter to "Stress!"

Dear STRESS,

You have made me believe for so long that I am messed up and have no command of my life. You are controlling and abusive physically, emotionally, and verbally. I am doing what I should have done long ago, and that is letting you go! I do NOT need you because you breakdown my body and you destroy my self-esteem and self-control! You are a part of the problem and not the solution! I will no longer let you manipulate me into being miserable! I will not miss you or receive people you send as your messengers! Enough is Enough, God's got my back! I will no longer live with stress brooding over things that I cannot change or control. I receive the word that "I AM TOO BLESSED TO BE STRESSED." God is in control and HE will guide and order my steps. Good bye and good riddance stress!

P.S. there is a no return address for this letter.

Has anyone has ever told you or convinced you to feel like your life won't amount to anything? The satiations and issues of your day seem to bring pressure, stress and more stress? I want you to know today, that no matter how much you're going through. Your story is NOT going to end like this! God Almighty is constantly writing your life's script and HE has NOT put the pen down yet! Understand that every breaking point has a breaking point. That means that everything which seems to bring pressure in your life has a place where it must cease and let up because "TROUBLE DON'T LAST ALWAYS!" The rain stops, the sun comes out and brings a brighter day! Now that is something to SHOUT about!! I pray blessings upon your life!

"I'm so sick and tired of this job!!

It's too much and I can't get it all done!!
"I have so many bills to pay, I don't have enough money…. I don't know what to do!!"
"I can't get anyone to help me! I need help now!"

What do these scenarios sound like?? People who are STRESSED! Stress is a burden that we carry; it's time to RELEASE some things!! 1 Peter 5:7 says, "Casting all your care upon him; for he cares for you." Stress is a weight! The "weight" itself isn't the problem. The problem unfolds when you HOLD ON to that weight! The longer you hold it, the heavier it becomes! Well, I go to a therapist anytime I feel stress coming on…. yes, Lisa goes to a therapist! You want to know my therapist name…. His name is JESUS! He has taught me how to pray!! Philippians 46 says, "Be fretful for nothing, but in everything by prayer and supplication, with thanksgiving, let your requests be made known to God, and the peace of God… will keep your hearts and minds through Christ Jesus." Jesus…#1 Stress Reliever! I pray blessings upon your life!

MY FIVE REASONS NOT TOO STRESS:

1. STRESS ONLY HURTS THE PERSON WHO IS STRESSING, STOP NOW!
2. STRESS RAISES BLOOD PRESSURE, NERVES, ANXIETY, DEPRESSION; RESEARCH PROVES STRESS WILL KILL YOU.
3. STRESS WILL NOT ALLOW YOU TO HAVE PEACE and HAPPINESS, STRESS HARASSES YOU TO THINK THE WORSE.
4. STRESS KEEPS YOU FOCUSING ON WHAT HAS NOT HAPPENED, OR THE WRONG PERSPECTIVE OF WHAT MAY BE HAPPENING.
5. FERVENT PRAYER IS A "STRESS RELIEVER!"

THE BEST

KEEP ON HOLDING ON! Whatever you are going through is ONLY for a season! God is going to see you through! The "giants" in your life may be big, but God is BIGGER! Where YOU are weak, God is STRONG! You may have failed, but God remains FAITHFUL! Say to yourself, "THE BEST IS YET TO COME! I CAN DO THIS BECAUSE GOD HAS A PLAN FOR MY LIFE! I HAVE TO KEEP THE FAITH AND TRUST GOD!" Matthew 21:22, "And all things, whatsoever ye shall ask in prayer, believing, ye shall receive." When God answers your prayer, He is increasing your FAITH. If there is a delay, He is increasing your patience. If He doesn't answer, believe He has you waiting on something so much BETTER for you! NEVER GIVE UP ON YOUR LIFE! THE BEST FOR YOU IS YET TO COME!! I pray blessings upon your life!

TRUST GOD

STAY ENCOURAGED and don't be frustrated into depression by what's going on around you, by what's not working out, or what's not coming together for you. It's just a SET UP by God to show you how to trust and depend on Him. He's bringing it all together, all around YOU and JUST for YOU, that NO man will be able to claim that they did it for you! Stand in faith and believe God and watch HIM work it out! Psalm: 121: 2 " I will lift up my eyes …. My help comes from the LORD, which made heaven and earth. "HE WILL WORK IT UP!! TRUST HIM!! I pray blessings upon your life!

Maximize this moment ...

The moment you take the time to think of, pray for, and bless someone else!!

VICTORY

GOD PLANNED FOR YOU TO OVERCOME, EVEN BEFORE THERE WERE OBSTACLES! WHEN YOU WERE IN YOUR MOTHER'S WOMB HE CHOSE YOU TO HAVE SUCCESS. HE WANTED US TO BE WINNERS AND NOT LOSERS, MAKERS AND NOT FAKERS, ABOVE AND NOT BENEATH! IF YOU LAST YOU CAN PASS, IF YOU CAN TAKE IT YOU CAN MAKE IT, AND IF YOU PRAY YOU WILL GO ALL THE WAY! I PRAY BLESSINGS UPON YOUR LIFE!

Victory Is Mine!!!

Worrying

What do you do when your house is being taken away, can't pay a bill, wondering what you and your children are going to eat for the week, can't find a job, sickness is attacking your body...do you worry? That's what I did when I went through those things. I had to learn that worrying is "Negative Meditation."

When we worry, we keep thinking over and over again the same negative thought. Worrying is like praying for what you don't want! Don't worry about anything! Instead, pray about everything!!

I'm a LIVING WITNESS THAT IT WORKED FOR ME! "WORRYING IS NOT ON MY "TO DO LIST" TODAY!" "SADNESS WILL NOT TAKE OVER MY SMILE!" " I CAN'T, IS NOT A PART OF MY VOCABULARY!" THESE "downers", DON'T EXIST WHEN YOU KNOW WHO IS IN CONTROL! GOD IS IN CONTROL! I PRAY BLESSINGS UPON YOUR LIFE!

When we worry, we are showing that we believe more in our problems than God's promise! PRAISE and STRENGTH go hand in hand when faced with trying circumstances! When you give God PRAISE, He gives you STRENGTH!

When you thank God in advance for a favorable outcome; your faith in God to deliver you from or out of the hands of your enemies will keep you encouraged! Isaiah 40:31 says "But they that wait upon the LORD shall renew their strength; they shall mount up with wings as eagles; they shall run, and not be weary, and they shall walk, and not faint." Let not your hearts be troubled……. Have a "Worry-Free" life! I pray blessings upon your life!

LS

Maximize this moment ...

That amazing moment when you realize God will never give up on you! Psalm 145:8 says, "The LORD is gracious and compassionate; slow to anger and rich in love."

MY PRAYERS OF MOTIVATION
TO GET YOU
TROUGH THE ROUGH PLACES

Father God,

We're praising you through the trials! We let it go and give it to you! We walk by FAITH! We BELIEVE in YOUR Word! God, you are OUR source! You are worthy of All our PRAISES!! Create in us a clean heart and renew a right spirit within us! I cry out for those who are going through right now......lift their heart, spirits, and mind! Let them know that YOU are their source, strength, and peace!! Your Word says, "But they that wait upon the Lord shall renew their **STRENGTH**; they shall mount up with wings as eagles; they shall run, and not be weary, and they shall walk, and not faint." ON THIS DAY...WE THANK YOU! We PRAISE YOU! We PRAISE YOU FOR BEING THERE IN THE MIDST OF IT ALL! WE'RE BETTER, SO MUCH BETTER BECAUSE OF IT!! GOD, I THANK YOU FOR ANSWERING OUR PRAYERS AND GIVING US VICTORY!!! IN THE MIGHTY NAME OF JESUS! AMEN!

Father God,

I pray for those who are facing a storm in their lives! Help them keep their eyes on YOU! Sometimes they may feel like the storm will swallow them up, but I know YOU will help them stay above water! Let us remember that YOU are there to protect, watch over and care for them! They are NEVER alone! The problem is NEVER greater than YOU, God! I Thank YOU for this day! I Thank YOU for all the wonderful things YOU have done for us! I GIVE YOU ALL the PRAISE! IN JESUS NAME...IN JESUS NAME...IN JESUS NAME.AMEN

Father God,

I bind up every spirit of low self-esteem, depression, doubt, fear, suicide, oppression, control and manipulation, despair, old wounds, failure, hopelessness, and every negative spirit that has attacked and attached itself to you! In the name of **JESUS**, I bind it up TODAY and loose in our lives **YOUR VICTORY**! God, let your face shine upon them and give them back the **PEACE** and the **JOY** that has been lost! We recognize that this spirit is not of GOD, but from the enemy, and we rebuke it and refuse it right now in the name of **Jesus**!! Your Word says that if I come near to YOU....YOU will come near to me (James 4:8) and I believe that Word and now I stand on it in faith! We trust YOU as our deliverer, we trust YOU as our redeemer, we trust YOU as our restorer and we trust YOU as our comforter!! In the mighty name of **Jesus,** I pray and declare these things...AMEN!!

Father God,

I thank YOU for answered prayers on today! ONLY YOU GOD CAN ANSWER MY PRAYER! I praise YOU for answering my spoken and unspoken requests! ONLY YOU GOD DESERVES THE PRAISE! Let today be a day of total VICTORY for YOUR people!! ONLY YOU GOD GETS THE GLORY!! Open doors that were once closed and close doors that should not be open! NO ONE BUT YOU GOD GETS THE HONOR! Thank YOU for YOUR Grace and Mercy! NO ONE BUT YOU GOD CAN BE EVERYTHING TO ME! YOU have been better to us than we have been to ourselves! NO ONE BUT YOU GOD!! We walk by FAITH and not by sight! We trust YOU in everything big or small! NO ONE BUT YOU GOD!! When the prayers go up, the bless-er (will come down and bring blessings into your circumstance) NO ONE BUT YOU GOD, AND BESIDES YOU THERE IS NO OTHER GOD! AMEN!

Father God,

In the name of Jesus. I come before You with a Heart of Thanksgiving! I thank You for Your grace and mercy that is released each day! Each day that You allow us to see, each day that You allow us to breathe, is something for us to be grateful! I thank You for my family and extended family! I thank You for my friends and BLESS EACH AND EVERY ONE OF THEM! I thank

You in the midst of trials, You will once again show Your mercy! I thank You for blessing me with my health and life today! I give thanks to You because Your love endures forever! In the Mighty Name of Jesus...AMEN!

Father God,

WE want to thank YOU for what you have already done in OUR lives! WE are not going to wait until WE feel better or things look better, WE are thanking you right now, THIS DAY! WE are not going to wait until the pain in OUR body goes away, WE are thanking you right now! WE are not going to wait until OUR financial situation improves, WE are going to thank you right now! WE are not going to wait until WE get that job, WE are thanking you right now! WE are not going to wait until it happens because WE ARE THANKING YOU RIGHT NOW!! WE confess it! WE have FAITH to BELIEVE IT And it is so IN THE NAME OF JESUS!! Amen!!

Father God,

Thank YOU for another day to see YOUR goodness in my life. Help us to see ourselves the way YOU see us. Help us to see the plans YOU have for us so that we can be empowered by YOU to fulfill our destiny. Thank YOU for reminding us that when we think we're standing alone, we're not, YOU ARE WITH US. Thank YOU for being our hope in difficult times, and holding us up when we want to sit this one out. Help us to remember YOU are a very present help in times of trouble. I am thankful that abundance WILL flow toward us today! In Jesus Name, Amen

Father God,

Your word says we know that all things work together for good to them that love God, to them who are the called according to His purpose! We stand on your promise! We know that you have already worked it out! I ask that you protect and bless EVERY household! Thank you for keeping us safe from dangers seen and unseen! Thank you for being our shield and our protector! We thank you for answering our prayers! We know not only is it going to be done, but IT'S ALREADY DONE! We pray by FAITH, we speak it by FAITH, and we believe we receive by FAITH! In Jesus name, we pray, AMEN!

Father God,

I pray for those who are facing a storm in their lives! Help them keep their eyes on YOU! Sometimes they may feel like the storm will swallow them up, but I know YOU will help them stay above water! Let us remember that YOU are there to protect, watch over and care for them! They are NEVER alone! The problem is NEVER greater than YOU God! I Thank YOU for this day! I Thank YOU for all the wonderful things YOU have done for us! I GIVE YOU ALL the PRAISE!!! IN JESUS NAME....IN JESUS NAME....AMEN!

Father God,

WE thank YOU for waking a brand-new day! Each day is a new day of PURPOSE, NEW BEGINNING, and a new day of MERCIES! God, I pray that YOU open doors that NO man can shut! WE ask that YOU close doors that YOU did not open! YOU know the plan for OUR lives! WE will NOT give up or quit for WE know OUR breakthrough is on the way!!! GLORY!!! God, YOU are ALWAYS on time!! YOU ...are OUR "ALL and ALL" The MOST HIGH GOD, A HEALER, JEHOVAH RAPHA, THE LORD WILL PROVIDE, JEHOVAH JIREH!!! WE know that when the PRAISES go UP, the BLESSINGS come down! WE thank you for being there when no one else was around!! WE BELIEVE IT AND RECEIVE IT ON THIS DAY!! IN THE NAME OF JESUS!! AMEN!!

Father God,

YOU know OUR hearts! When days and nights go by and it seems like no change is taking place, and WE fall into deep despair. WE pray that you let your **PEACE** fall upon US! Fill OUR heart with the **HOPE** that OUR lives are in YOUR hands! Lift the pain from US and allow YOUR **JOY** to flow freely through US!!! AMEN!

APPENDIX A

Power Steps I Used to Make a Positive and Fulfilling Lifestyle Change

"The doctor has told me once again my sugar and blood pressure are both up, my cholesterol is high and I need to lose about 50lbs. I love to eat; maybe I'll start making those **changes** at the beginning of next year." (It's March of the current year)

Friend: "Did he beat you again? You need to leave! Why didn't you call the police? Why didn't you call me! You need to go to the hospital; it looks like your arm is broken!!

Victim: "I know…. but I love him. He provides for me and the children. I just have to stop doing those things that displease him. He's all I got…he's the first man to really love me."

Friend: "No, you got God and you have me! God will provide! You must make a **change** right now! Let me help you!

"I'm not making enough money on this job. I've been working here for years and I've never received a raise. Look for another job? **Changing** what I'm doing is too much of a hassle. (Sighs) I guess I'll just stay here and deal with it."

CHANGE……. Why do we cringe at times when we need to make a change? Do we enjoy the "comfort zone" that we are in? Are we afraid people may not like us? Is the transition just too much work and effort`? You've tried from time-to-time to make certain changes in your life, but sometimes the changes weren't successful. That's because Change is not easy! It's hard but in the long run, the reward is worth it.

A successful change works better when it becomes a positive habit incorporated into your lifestyle. A Lifestyle Change requires a commitment and guts to see it through. Of course, it's a process that takes time, a determined attitude and self-discipline, but you must see it through. Let's look at the **"Power Steps to a Lifestyle Change"** I've created for myself, and I am happy to share with others:

Power Step #1-PRAY

Power Step # 2-RENEW YOUR MIND

Power Step # 3- DISCOVER PURPOSE IN LIFE

Power Step # 4-JUST DO IT POWER STEP

Power Step # 5- SHARE WITH OTHERS

Power Step #1-PRAY

Prayer is a tremendous part of my everyday living. However, it becomes even more essential when you are attempting to change and achieve a higher goal. Our lives consist of making daily decisions that affect ourselves and those we care about. In making some of those decisions, we may at times, act and think too quickly without consultation or resolve. Hindsight being 20/20, we come to realize that we should have waited and sought higher counsel. So why not include the higher source and the universal intelligence that knows all and is all, which is GOD. Prayer involves you putting God's wisdom and instruction into the circumstance and listening to his voice. Before you act, give it over to God in prayer. God will speak to you at the core of your being and let you know what and how to do. Embrace and accept the Word that God gives you. Not only will He speak to you but He will show you how to perceive, navigate, and take charge of you in any situation.

Power Step # 2-RENEW YOUR MIND

When you become a Christian, the "old man" aka, the old nature dies within you, and you are "spiritually" reborn and awaken. You then become one with Jesus Christ and you are admonished to renew your mind from your previous way of thinking and doing. I also believe that we can embark on physical situations and circumstances in our life that calls for us to renew our mind and once again change our system and approach to how we do things.

When I was diagnosed with lupus, it was devastating and life-shattering news that would affect the rest of my life. I didn't realize at the time that my fatigue and low-energy level coincided with my immune system trying to shut-down. When the doctor explained the effects lupus would have on my body, I instantly knew I had to make a change concerning my health. But how could I in my devastated condition? I knew I needed to get my mind right and change my health condition but not just a temporary fix, my whole health system and wellness philosophy needed to be overhauled; a lifestyle change is what it would take.

To make that change, I knew I would have to renew my mind. This means changing the way you think and look at things. When you change your perspective about something, it also changes your attitude, ideas, opinion and even your desires. Renewing your mind is never just a "one-time" event; it's a healthy and essential part of lifestyle change that begins in constant communication with Jesus Christ. Philippians 2:5 "Let this mind be in you, which was also in Christ Jesus."

Power Step # 3- Discover PURPOSE IN YOUR LIFE

The purpose for our lives was given to us when we were young children. Values such as: going to school, making good grades, graduating, going to church, etc. So, my question is, "What is YOUR Purpose?" Do you know or are you waiting for someone to tell you? Guess what, no one can "tell" you the purpose for your life. YOU must find your purpose and VALIDATE it to and for yourself.

By doing this, you take ownership of this, your God given purpose. You then have an inner drive to move toward fulfilling everything that pertains to your purpose. If you haven't found or don't know your purpose, make it your "Purpose" to find out. How do you do that?

Go back and read Power Step # 1. PRAY. Pray and ask God to show you what your purpose is in life. When you pray, be sincere and faithful in the answer that is given to you. Don't fear or avoid the path of finding purpose in your life; it may seem like an overwhelming task, but God will never leave you nor forsake! Purpose is the main objective behind you setting the goals you want to achieve. When God reveals your purpose to you, OWN IT, LIVE IN IT, and BECOME IT! Then watch as your life unfolds around it.

Power Step # 4-JUST DO IT

I've always loved the Nike commercials famous for telling us to "Just do it!" but it became very significant to me. My goal to lose weight started with a desire that became a purpose. Once I knew my purpose, I determined in my mind to make some changes. I changed what I ate and incorporated exercise in my life. This is a lifestyle change for me...not a "One-Stop Shop" diet. I adopted the saying, "Just Do It!"

Some years ago, I wanted to start my own Personalized Children's Book business. I was excited about the thought of it and I knew I had to create a plan to get it started. Not once did I think: my books won't sell, I don't have enough start-up money, or I just couldn't do it.

I had a need =my motivation

I prayed= my stabilization

I had a positive mindset = my determination

I knew what my next step was, just do it Lisa!

My demonstration was to "Just Do It!"

When I went through a divorce, it was devastating and an emotional time in my life. I had to make changes in order to take care of myself and most importantly, my daughters. Depression, confusion, anger, hate, low self-esteem, no drive, and no resolve took over my life. I thank God I had just a grain of mustard-seed FAITH to call on His name, in the midst of the bucket-full of tears I had begun to shed on a daily basis. One day I woke up and I said, "no more tears!" I looked in the mirror and declared, "I will live and not die!" I remember that moment so vividly in my mind and that's when a great transformation took place!

I went to a local college and signed up to take classes to get my Associate's degree to better my life. *"Just Do It!"* Being out of school so long made it tough, but God gave me a willing heart and a positive mindset! I had to tell myself many times, *"Just Do It!"* I desired to have certifications in my area of study. I continued going to school until I got them by praying and telling myself, *"Just Do It!"* I desired to get a Bachelor's degree. Working hard, studying, and making it through two surgeries along the way saying, "Lisa, you can do this!" I desired to get my Master's degree but working two jobs and with a lot of prayers, I kept saying, "Lisa, you are almost there!" *"Just Do It!"* Allowing the inner writer in me to come out and finally start to write a book…. while saying, "Lisa, you are doing it!" Obstacles, test, and trials will come, but never give up on your dreams, your goals, or your Purpose!
"Just Do It!"

Power Step # 5- Share With Others

"I'm just going to help my four, and no more!" Wow, what a limited way to live! It's so easy to be consumed with your own life, your own self and your own family until you just don't take the time to share with others. You may be wondering, why should I share with others when I am attempting to change my life? When we are making a lifestyle change, you don't do it on your own. As you bless others along the way, they in turn will help you to make your load lighter. We bless others through our actions, our kindness, and even sharing our stories.

Genesis 12 says, And I will bless them that bless thee. So along your journey, be sure to bless others, even when you don't feel like it. When we stop to bless others, and take the focus off ourselves, our lives become fuller and richer. Have a mindset to lift others up and it will, in turn, lift you. Blessing others doesn't always mean giving something monetary. It can be your smile, a kind word, prayer or even giving a little of your time. It is a great gift from within when you put yourself on hold on and decide to be a blessing to someone else. Ralph Waldo Emerson said, "...we can never help another without helping ourselves."

Your desire for a LIFESTYLE CHANGE must be greater than your desire to remain the SAME! Now think about it, if we put as much energy into changing, as we do in trying to keep things to remain the SAME, we would be on our way to discovering something so amazing, so well worth changing for; that it would make you wonder why you fought CHANGE in the first place!

Embarking on a Lifestyle Change will require and create growth. Growth that could produce greater joy, greater health, greater love, greater wealth, and an overall greater life! I pray you embrace my **Power Steps for a Positive and Fulfilling Lifestyle Change,** make them your own and tailor them for your life. I speak blessings upon you!

APPENDIX B

Self-Worth &Self-Esteem

How do we obtain it? What do you think about yourself? Do you sometimes compare yourselves with others? Do you feel that you are making a difference? Is your self-esteem high or low? Are you a person of worth and value? Just a few questions to think about as set forth some definitions of Self-worth and self-esteem.

Self-Worth is the opinion you have about you and the value you place on yourself. An example of self-worth is your belief that you are a good person who deserves good things or your belief that you are a bad person who deserves bad things.

Self Esteem is a confidence and satisfaction in oneself; a feeling of delight in yourself and your accomplishments. I will be using these terms interchangeably because there meanings are so closely knitted. While your esteem has to do with your belief in who you are and what you can achieve, your worth incorporates your self-esteem and how you value of yourself.

Your self-worth meter started when you were a young child. How you felt as a child and your parents/ family, and friend's support of you, or lack thereof, contributed to your self- worth. The way you perceive yourself, the way you talk about yourself, and the way you present yourself, are insights about your esteem. If your self-worth is not positive, then you experience low self-esteem. It doesn't help when others put us down or tell us that we won't amount to anything.

As a child at the age of ten, I lost my mother. She was an essential, nurturing and loving person in my life. My father was never around and I was an only child. Any "positive" self-worth I had gathered, was lost when she died. While growing up I would learn to love myself and yes, "learning to love yourself is one of the greatest loves of all", because how can you love others when you do not love yourself?

I didn't know that God was teaching me this all along. I learned to show myself love by treating MYSELF with care, compassion, forgiveness, and respect. Genesis 1:26-27 says we are made in His image, the very image of God, Psalm 139 says we are fearfully and wonderfully made, confirming God's prior knowledge and plan for us to know and understand our true greatness for which we were created.

Our self-worth sometimes is usually based on what others tell us about ourselves. Often times, you try to live up to what others want you to be. When you do this, you defiantly hinder your self-esteem by trying to live up to someone else's changing perspective of you. You are living in the expectations of others and not of God. Don't allow what people say, think or do to you, bring your self-esteem down!

True self-worth comes from God: "I can do all things through Christ which strengthens me" Philippians 4:13. If Satan can rob us of our self-worth, then he can hinder us so that we don't accomplish the works of God and become the things we are destined to be. Tell yourself that you are relevant and that you do matter! You must become your own cheerleader.

Have pep-talks with yourself that are encouraging, motivating and uplifting! "I am somebody! I have a purpose! I can do it! I'm beautiful! I'm handsome! I'm smart! I will make a difference!" Speak it, Claim it, Believe it, Receive it, And BE it!

What things can you identify in your life that brought your self-esteem down? Working on a job for years and you are up for a promotion, then a new hire comes in and takes the spot that was meant for you. Your self-worth/self-esteem takes a big hit because of it. Now you're feeling like you're not good enough, but your evaluations say that you're an excellent employee. You've received "Employee of the Month" ten times in ten years. You go "beyond-the-call-of-duty" on the job and the promotion you've been waiting for now belongs to someone else.

You've been in a marriage that you thought would last forever. You've been the best spouse you know how to be and you lived up to the vows that were sanctified by God and then you find out your significant other has cheated on you. Your self-worth hits rock bottom. You lose your house and your car in the same month, you haven't a clue what to do. You now feel worthless and lost.

These things and situations like these can cause you to have a low self-esteem and no self-worth. Have you ever thought that God might have something better in store for you, and these situations are just tools to bring you to the better? The enemy's job is to convince us that our efforts are worthless and we don't matter. To make us give up and believe that everything we've worked for is no good and hopeless. Instead of dwelling on Satan's "down-grades," let's improve, and UPGRADE!

Claim the promises of God: "My grace is sufficient for thee: for my strength is made perfect in weakness. Most gladly, therefore, will I rather glory in my infirmities, that power of Christ may rest upon me." II Corinthians 12:9.

Don't allow a let-down, cause a break-down and you become broken-down. God says when you are weak, He is strong! STAND-UP, REJOICE-UP, and be LIFTED-UP for what God is doing in your life! Focus on positive things and see every circumstance and situation, whether good or bad, as an opportunity to increase your God empowered self-worth and self-esteem.

We need healthy self-esteem and self-worth in our life, therefore adopt an "I CAN" attitude and eliminate negative self-talk from your vocabulary. Your life has a purpose and you can be anything you want to be!

My positive self-worth prayer is:

Walk with me Lord, expand my territory, open up my heart, put me where I need to be, let me learn the lessons that I need to learn, point me in the right direction and I shall go, because without you I'm nothing and with you I am UNSTOPPABLE!! BELIEVE IT AND RECEIVE IT! AMEN!

I want to encourage you to believe in YOU because when God is for you, He is more than the world against you! Don't allow anyone to steal your joy! You are "Worthy" your "Esteem" is mighty through God!

I pray blessings upon your life!
Much Love!

LISA SOLOMON

http://www.thesolomonsreflection.com/

Bring Me To Your Next Event!

Minister Lisa Solomon

If you need a panelist for your forum, speaker for your seminar or host for your next workshop,

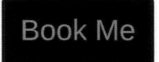

https://www.facebook.com/lgtech?fref=ts

https://twitter.com/ldgtech

lgtech0314@gmail.com

http://thesolomonsreflection.com (website)

STRENGTH FROM THE LION'S DEN with host Apostle John L. Solomon on www.blogtalkradio.com/weinspirenetworkradio is a compelling, eclectic talk show that discusses life's difficult situations, relevant current topics, poignant issues, and empowering stories from a biblical perspective. It is a beacon of hope, a source of meditative knowledge, enthusiastic listening motivation, and fun; addressed by an interesting array of thought leaders, musical ministers, celebrated personalities, and odds- defying difference makers.

FINALLY, a program that brings the medicinal effects of humor, transcendent Godly wisdom, the efficacy of education, but primarily strength and hope to the weary from the source-hood of our connection with our Lord Christ. Apostle John L. Solomon I am going to power up broken people: men, women, boys, and girls who need strength, prophetic encouragement, is someone who identifies with pain and will show you how to get up and stay up.